Hats
and
Other Headwear

Jane Bingham

WAYLAND

First published in 2008 by Wayland

Copyright © Wayland 2008

Wayland
338 Euston Road
London NW1 3BH

Wayland Australia
Level 17/207 Kent Street
Sydney NSW 2000

Senior editor: Joyce Bentley
Designer: Holly Fullbrook
Picture researcher: Kathy Lockley

British Library Cataloguing in Publication Data
Bingham, Jane
        Hats and other headwear. - (Clothes around the world)
        1. Headgear - Juvenile literature
        I. Title
        391.4'3

ISBN 978 0 7502 5313 0

Picture acknowledgements:
Richard Cooke/Alamy: 20; P. Deliss/Godong/Corbis: 22; Chad Ehlers/Alamy: 4, 21;
Werner Forman/Corbis: 9; Chuck Franklin/Alamy: 27; Tim Graham/Alamy: 3, 11,
25; Jan Halaska/Alamy: 16; Holmes Garden Photos/Alamy: 10; Jeremy
Horner/Panos Pictures: 14; Image State/Alamy: 15; Stan Kujawa/Alamy: 24;
Lebrecht Music & Arts Photo Library/Alamy: 8; Life Images/Alamy: 26
Gerd Ludwig/Visum/Panos Pictures: 6; Jenny Matthews/Alamy: 7; Jenny
Matthews/Panos Pictures: 18; Eric Miller/Panos Pictures: 23; NASA-HQ-GRIN: title
page, 19; Sean Sprague/Panos Pictures: 12; Jack Sullivan/Alamy: 17; John
Sylvester/Alamy: 13; Horacio Villalobos/Corbis: 5

Printed in China

Wayland is a division of Hachette Children's Books,
an Hachette Livre UK company.

Contents

Why do people wear hats?

People wear hats to protect their heads. When it's sunny, a hat can stop your head from getting burnt. When it's cold, wearing a thick hat will help to keep you warm. A hard hat can protect your head if you fall, or if something falls on you.

Some cosy hats keep your head warm and protect your ears from the cold as well!

If you wear a cap with a peak, it will shade your eyes and stop you being dazzled by the sun. A hat with a wide brim will keep your whole face in the shade.

Some people wear hats as part of a uniform. But often people choose a hat just because it looks good!

It Works!

Baseball caps

Baseball caps are very useful for sport. The cap has a large peak that shades the eyes so players can spot a ball, even in bright light. Baseball caps have a strap at the back that can be tightened to make the cap fit well. This means that the cap doesn't fall off, even when a player is running.

Hats around the world

People around the world have many different types of headwear. Often, their hats are specially suited to the weather in their country.

In Russia and Canada, where it can be cold and snowy, people wear fur hats to keep their heads warm. In the mountains of Peru, people make warm hats from wool. These cosy woollen hats have flaps to keep the ears warm.

This Russian mother and child are keeping their heads warm and dry, even in the snow.

In dry, sunny countries, such as Spain, people often wear a light straw hat with a shady brim. Some Mexican men wear straw sombreros with very wide brims. The sombrero brim is so wide, it can shade the whole of the wearer's body.

Arabs in the desert wear a long cotton **headdress**, fixed with a band around the head. The headdress protects the wearer's head and neck from the sun.

It Works!

Keeping off the rain

In the rice fields of China, farmers often have to work in the rain. They wear pointed hats with wide, sloping sides. The hat works like a small umbrella, keeping the rain well away from the farmer's face.

The history of hats and headwear

Thousands of years ago, people kept warm by covering their heads with animal skins. In warmer parts of the world, they made simple hats from reeds or leaves.

In ancient Egypt, many people wore wigs made from thick black hair or wool. The wigs were decorated with beads and jewels.

Egyptian queens wore tall crowns with simple decorations. The crowns made them look very elegant.

Weird and Wonderful

Fish helmets

The Romans made metal helmets for their soldiers. They also made some helmets that looked like fish. Fish helmets were worn by **gladiators**, who were forced to fight each other as an entertainment. Gladiators in fish helmets were called murmillos, or 'fish men'.

Mayan headdresses were carved with fierce animal faces. They made the chiefs look very powerful.

The Maya people lived in Mexico two thousand years ago. Their chiefs wore tall headdresses, with colourful feathers sprouting from the top.

In **medieval times**, kings and queens wore golden crowns that glittered with jewels.

Some medieval women wore a very tall, pointed hat. The hat was shaped like a long, narrow cone, and it had a veil fixed to the top.

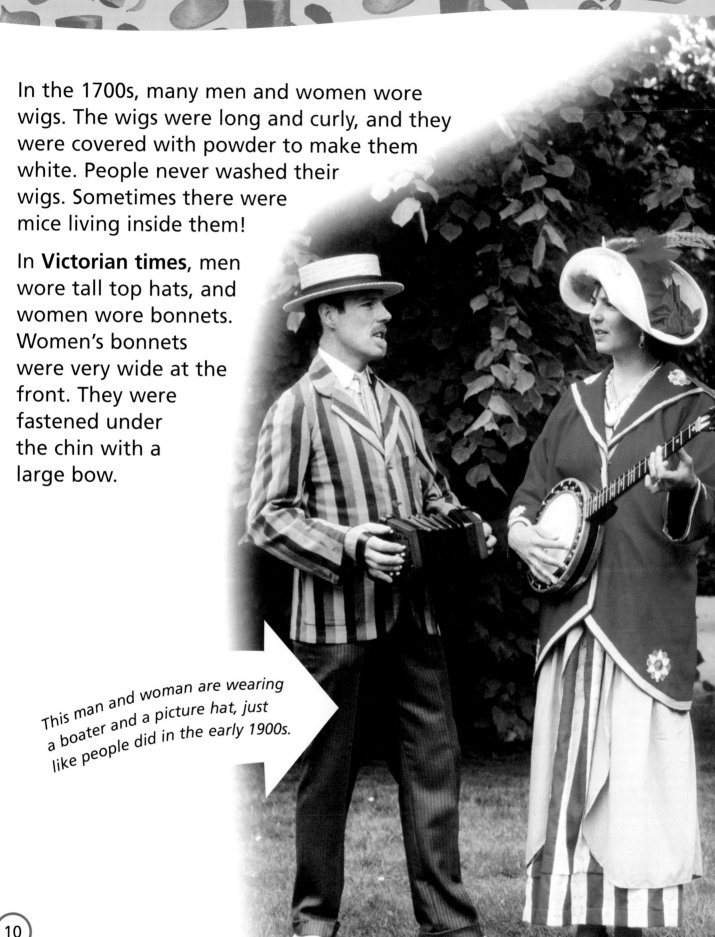

In the 1700s, many men and women wore wigs. The wigs were long and curly, and they were covered with powder to make them white. People never washed their wigs. Sometimes there were mice living inside them!

In **Victorian times**, men wore tall top hats, and women wore bonnets. Women's bonnets were very wide at the front. They were fastened under the chin with a large bow.

This man and woman are wearing a boater and a picture hat, just like people did in the early 1900s.

In the early 1900s, men wore straw hats with a flat top and a wide brim. The hats were called boaters because men wore them when they went rowing in boats on the river.

Women wore large picture hats. Picture hats were decorated with ribbons and feathers, and artificial fruit. Some women even had a stuffed bird in their picture hats!

Flashback

Fifties fascinators
Fascinators are tiny hats that women attach to their hair. They are usually made from feathers and net. They were first worn in the 1950s, but then they went out of fashion. Now they are popular again.

What are hats made from?

For thousands of years, hats have been made from natural materials, like wool, cotton or leather. Now, some hats are made from new materials, such as plastic.

Wool is a very useful material for hats. When it is knitted, it is slightly stretchy. So a woolly hat fits your head very snugly.

Many people today wear woollen **beanies**. Hats like this are made in a factory.

In the past, most children wore hand-knitted hats. Today, children still wear woollen hats, but they are usually not made by hand. Instead, the wool is knitted on a machine.

In cold, wet countries, people often wear hats made from fur or leather. Fur and leather are both **waterproof**, but there are other materials that keep the water out. Some people wear rain hats made from plastic. Fishermen wear **sou'westers** made from a heavy plastic, called PVC.

In France, felt berets are often worn by men.

In hot, sunny countries, people make straw hats. They weave the hats from narrow strips of straw. Straw hats have hundreds of tiny holes to let air through so your head stays cool.

Hats made from cotton also keep you cool. Cotton can be made into a long, flowing headdress, like the ones Arabs wear in the desert. It can also be wound around the head to make a **turban**.

*Some Arab headdresses have a **traditional** pattern of red and white.*

In the past, people wore metal helmets to protect their heads. But metal is very uncomfortable to wear. Now most helmets are made from plastic that is light but very tough.

Swimmers wear caps made from very thin rubber. Swimming caps fit your head so tightly that your hair stays dry, even when you swim underwater!

Wearing a rubber cap makes your head more **streamlined** so you can swim faster through the water.

Headwear for work

Many people have a special hat for work. Some workers wear hats to protect themselves. Other work hats make it easier for people to do their job. Wearing a special hat makes workers look smart, and can make them feel good about their job!

Weird and Wonderful

Wigs for work!
Imagine having to wear a long, curly wig to work! Sometimes people wear a wig when they take part in a **ceremony**. It may seem weird at first, but they wear the wig for a reason. It reminds everyone that the ceremony is very old.

Some workers wear a hat to keep their hair tidy. Chefs have tall white hats that cover most of their hair, keeping it well away from the food. Surgeons wear a special cap when they perform an operation. The cap covers all of their hair, so no dirt or germs can escape.

Some hats make workers easy to recognize. For example, police officers usually wear a special cap. This makes them easy to spot in an emergency.

Surgeons wear a new cap for each operation. Afterwards, the caps are thrown away.

Headwear for protection and safety

Some headwear is specially designed to keep people safe. People who work on building sites wear hard hats made from very tough plastic. Their hard hat helps to protect them if something heavy falls on their head, or if they have an accident.

Miners working underground wear a special helmet to protect them from falling rocks. Miners' helmets have a lamp fixed on the front so the miners can see ahead of them, when they are working in the dark.

What Would You Wear?

What kind of headwear would you wear if you had to climb a muddy cliff in the rain?

A. A baseball cap
B. A fisherman's sou'wester
C. A lightweight hard hat
D. A woollen beanie

(Answer on page 31)

The lamp on this miner's helmet has a cable that leads to a battery on his belt.

When astronauts travel in space, they need a space helmet to keep them alive. It is impossible to breathe the air in space, so the helmet is very tightly sealed. **Oxygen** from an air tank is pumped into the helmet so the astronaut can breathe normally.

In this picture, the astronaut's helmet looks like a mirror. But the astronaut can still see out.

Headwear for sport

People often wear special headwear for sports – especially if their sport puts them in danger.

Motorcyclists, climbers and cyclists all wear helmets to protect their heads. Some sports players need to protect their faces as well as their heads. American football players wear a helmet with bars covering the face.

It Works!

Bicycle helmet

Bicycle helmets are very strong and tough, but they are also light and comfortable. They are padded inside and they can be adjusted to fit your head exactly. Modern helmets have a lot of **ventilation holes**. This means you can keep a cool head while you cycle!

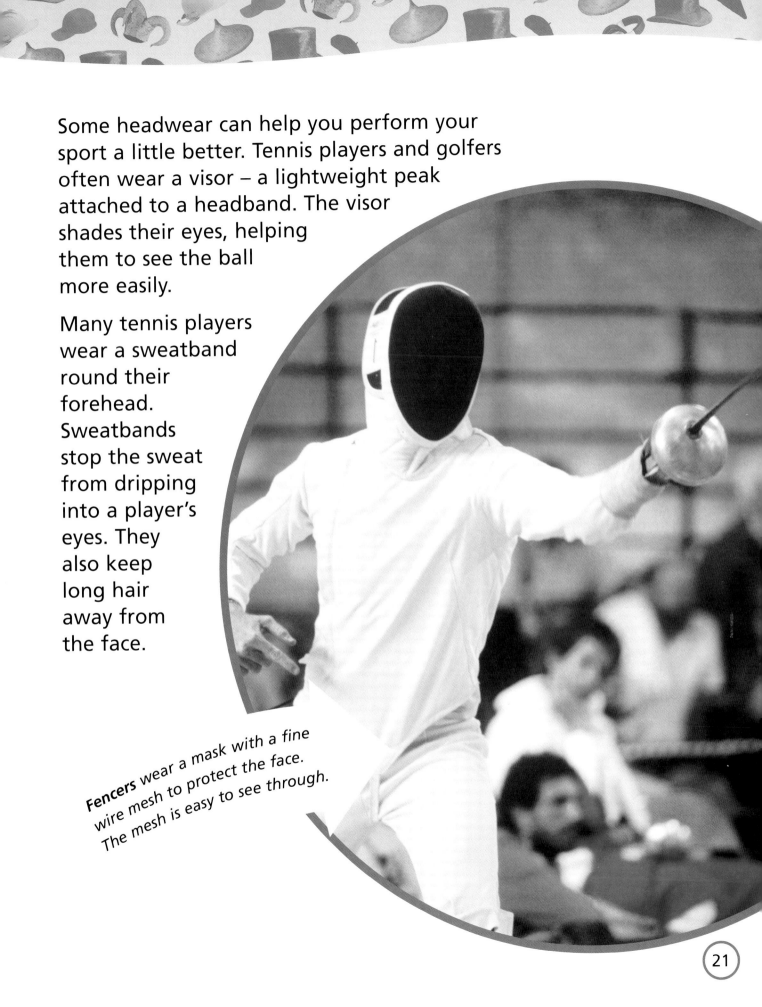

Some headwear can help you perform your sport a little better. Tennis players and golfers often wear a visor – a lightweight peak attached to a headband. The visor shades their eyes, helping them to see the ball more easily.

Many tennis players wear a sweatband round their forehead. Sweatbands stop the sweat from dripping into a player's eyes. They also keep long hair away from the face.

Fencers wear a mask with a fine wire mesh to protect the face. The mesh is easy to see through.

Religious headwear

People often wear a special head covering as a sign of their religion. When people wear a religious head covering they are showing respect to their God.

Jewish boys and men wear a **kippah**. This is a small cap without a peak.

Many Muslim girls and women wear a headscarf that covers their hair and neck. This head-covering is known as the **hijab**.

Jewish boys wear a kippah when they attend religious classes.

Flashback

Headwear with history

Most religious headwear has a very long history. It has stayed unchanged for hundreds of years. When people wear their special headwear, they are reminded of the long history of their religion.

Sikh men and boys often wear a turban. Boys start to wear a turban after a special ceremony. The turban-tying ceremony takes place when a boy is around 13 years old.

The leaders of religions often have special headwear. For example, in the Christian Church, **archbishops** wear a tall pointed hat, called a mitre.

An archbishop's mitre makes him stand out from the crowd.

Hats for special occasions

People love to wear a hat for a special occasion. When you dress up in a hat, it puts you in the mood to celebrate!

All around the world, people wear special headwear for **carnivals**. Often, a carnival is a good excuse to dress up and celebrate. But in some countries, carnivals are more traditional. People take part in dances wearing painted masks, just like their **ancestors** did thousands of years ago.

People wear amazing hats for carnival parades.

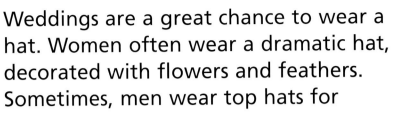

Weddings are a great chance to wear a hat. Women often wear a dramatic hat, decorated with flowers and feathers. Sometimes, men wear top hats for a wedding.

Brides at weddings sometimes have a veil covering their face. In Japanese weddings, the bride wears a large hat shaped like a boat.

Hats for fun

Hats come in all sorts of shapes and sizes. They can be brightly coloured, and they can be decorated in amazing ways.

Dressing up in a silly hat is lots of fun. You can wear a hat with floppy rabbit ears, or a cap that's covered with dinosaur spikes. You can try on a giant, squashy top hat. Or you can choose a hat that looks like a small, furry animal!

Flashback

Jester's hat

In medieval times, **jesters** wore a colourful hat with two or three long points. At the end of each point was a bell. As the jester danced around, the bells on the hat jingled. Today, people still wear jester hats for fun.

This surprising hat also works as a float. With a hat like this, you can lie back in the water and relax!

Some hats are full of surprises. There are hats that squirt water and hats with flashing lights. There are even caps with a small propeller fixed on top. When the wind blows, the propeller spins around, like a tiny helicopter.

Make your own jester's hat

To make a jester's hat you will need some soft fabric in two different colours. Two old T-shirts work especially well. You will also need three small bells. Most sewing and craft shops sell bells.

You will need
2 pieces of soft fabric, measuring at least 40cm x 40cm ★ 3 small bells ★ large sheet of paper (A1 size) ★ scissors ★ pins ★ blunt needle ★ thread ★ marker pen

1. Ask an adult to help you draw your hat shape on the paper, as shown. Cut around the hat shape, leaving about 2 cm around the edges.

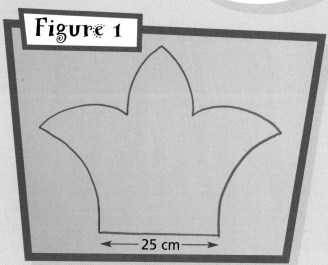

Figure 1

←— 25 cm —→

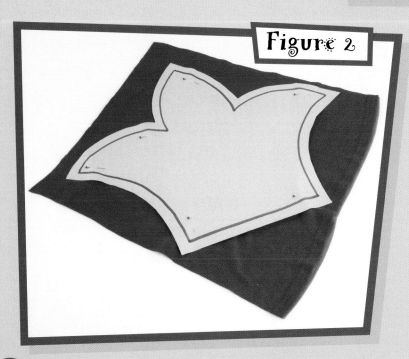

Figure 2

2. Lay the two pieces of fabric, one on top of the other, with their best sides facing inwards. Then ask an adult to pin the paper pattern on top of the fabric. Carefully cut around the hat shape then take out the pins. You will have two matching fabric hat shapes.

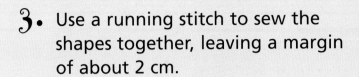

3. Use a running stitch to sew the shapes together, leaving a margin of about 2 cm.

Figure 3

4. Turn your hat the right way out, so all the sewing is on the inside. Then sew a bell at the end of each point. Stuff the hat with newspaper or cloth to give it shape.

Figure 4

Your jester's hat is ready to wear! Put the hat on your head and fold over the base.

Dress-up box

Dress for the desert in 5 minutes

In the desert, it is burning hot in the day and freezing cold at night. People dress for the desert in long, loose robes and sandals. They wear a cotton headdress that covers their head and neck.

To create your own desert clothing, you will need sandals and something long and loose to wear. You will also need a drying up cloth and a headband to fix it to your head. (Use a tie if you don't have a headband.)

1. Fix the cloth firmly on your head with a headband.

2. Tuck the sides of the cloth into the headband.

3. You could add some sunglasses and flip-flops to complete the costume.

Glossary

ancestors – people who have died who are related to someone who is living

archbishop – a leading priest in the Christian Church

beanie – a small hat which fits closely to the head

carnival – a celebration. Some carnivals are part of a religious festival.

ceremony – words, actions and/or music to mark a special occasion

fencer – a person who fights as a sport with a long thin sword

gladiators – Roman warriors who fought each other to entertain the public

headdress – a decorative head covering

hijab – an Arabic word for a scarf or veil, used by women to cover their head and shoulders

jester – someone who entertained people in medieval times

kippah – a small rounded cap worn by Jewish men and boys

medieval times – a period of history between the years 1000 and 1450

oxygen – a colourless gas in the air, that humans need to breathe in order to stay alive

reeds – plants with long, hollow stems that grow near water

Roman times – a period of history between BC 31 and AD 284

sou'wester – a waterproof hat with a wide brim at the back to keep the neck dry

streamlined – designed to move through air or water easily

traditional – used in the same way for hundreds of years

turban – a head covering made from a long piece of cloth wrapped around the head many times

ventilation holes – holes to allow air in and out

Victorian times – a period of English history between 1837 and 1901

waterproof – when an item of clothing is waterproof, it does not allow water to get through it

What would you wear?

Answer to the question on page 18.

When you are climbing a muddy cliff, you are at risk from falling rocks, especially when it is wet. You could also slip and fall and hurt your head. So you should definitely choose C – a lightweight hard hat. All the other choices would not protect your head, and you could be killed. Of course, it's never a good idea to climb a muddy cliff in the rain – even if you are wearing the right headwear!

Index

Photos or pictures are shown below in bold, **like this**.